2,001
Top Titles
&Tips
for over 285
common and not-so-common
Scrapbook Topics

Crystal Dawn Perry

ClearSky Publishing
Hixson, Tennessee

2,001
TOP TITLES
& Tips

A very special thanks to my mother, Pat and parents-in-law, Ernie and Sandy for their love, support, and baby-sitting "services." I must also thank them for the use of their computers after mine was struck by lightning (as luck would have it) ¾ of the way into writing this book. Also, thank you to my sister, Connie and my best friend, Paula who supported me from the beginning.

2,001 Top Titles & Tips.
ClearSky Publishing
P.O. Box 606-B Hixson, TN. 37343

ISBN 0-9706381-0-8

I dedicate this book to my beautiful daughter, Skyla, who graciously took her naps, allowing me to write and to my husband, Keith, the most perfect man I'll ever know.

Notes

Suggestions for getting the *most* out of 2,001 Top Titles & Tips:

1. You know the feeling... you've got the perfect photographs, the perfect papers, the most adorable stickers as well as die cuts, and maybe you've even arranged them on your page. Now, what are you going to title your layout? You want that one perfect word or phrase that will catch somcone's attention and draw them into the pictures and the story on the page; but you're drawing a blank.

Suppose your layout is of a birthday party. Naturally, the first topic you would turn to is "birthday". You may be happy with any one of the titles listed here but you could be missing out on a headline for your page that would sum up the day much better. Look at all possibilities... Was there a theme for the party (ex. "bears" or "dolls")? Maybe you want to remember the overwhelming number of "gifts"? If this was your child's first birthday party, you may be surprised to find the title you want listed under "firsts". You may still be most happy with the title you selected from the birthday list but to capture the memory, don't limit your options.

2. We've all gone to the scrapbook store with a specific theme in mind and ended up walking out with additional papers and stickers. We didn't know what we would do with them. We just bought them because they were pretty and we just had to have them. This book is great for inspiring ideas. What is on the paper? Flowers? Look up "flowers." Even if you don't find the title

you want, this will cross-reference you to "gardening." You don't have to be an avid gardener to find the perfect title here. *(Check out the cross-reference even if you don't think it applies to you, there is a reason for the reference and you may be surprised to find what you were looking for.)* For example, maybe when you see "Pickin' and Grinnin'", it reminds you of the pictures of your daughter picking flowers for you. This is the beginning of an adorable layout that you may not have otherwise thought of.

3. This idea also works for photographs that you want to use but you don't have an idea for. What element can you pull out of the photo? Is it a picture of your "daughter"? Is she surrounded by "toys" or maybe she's getting into "trouble"? Look up any of these options, or for the best selection, consider the titles listed under all of these topics. Before long, you'll be digging through your patterned paper and die cuts looking for just the right items to accessorize your next scrapbook layout.

4. While looking up topics for the pages or photos that you already have, you'll no doubt stumble across inspiration for layouts that you haven't yet planned. It's great when that happens. It gets you excited and anxious to do more pages. Unfortunately, there may be times when you find yourself in a creative lull. This is the perfect time to scan through the titles in this book. In fact, it's a good idea to do this anyway. By scanning through, you'll notice topics that you did not realize were here or that you wouldn't

have thought to look for. Don't forget, there are over 285 topics covered. You won't know what is here unless you look.

5. A final suggestion is to use all of the blank spaces in the book to your benefit. As you flip through the pages, you may be surprised that a simple phrase can spark so many ideas. Forget what you learned about not writing in books. This is your book now. Use the blank spaces located at the bottom of the pages to write down your ideas as you go. We all know how easy it is to forget an idea if we don't write it down the moment we think of it.

Notes

Tips to personalize your title:

As you look through this book, you'll notice italicized sentences under some topics. These are tips to help you personalize your title according to subject. If after using these tips and the suggestions in the previous section, you still don't have the title you want for your page, here are more ideas to help you come up with your own:

1. Use two or more words that start with the same letter. Try this with your subject's name or a special character trait.
ex.- Chandler the Chatterbox *or* Rowdy Riley

2. Use a quote overheard at the day's event. Was there something funny that everybody laughed at? If you write it down or use the punchline to title your page, you won't forget it years later; the way we unfortunately forget most of the things we hear.

3. Better yet, is there an expression or favorite saying that your subject often uses? Maybe an appropriate title for a page about your teenager would be "Cool" or "Whatever". This not only shows a little insight to your subject's personality but records a memory that will be interesting for generations to come. Wouldn't it tell a lot to future generations to see a page about their Great-Grandmother titled with her favorite saying?

4. Title a page with your subject's nickname. It may be something that everybody calls this person or it may be a nickname that's exclusively from you. Although you know what the nickname is, other people looking at your album or future generations may not. You may even forget about it years later. If you have a special name you call your baby or young child, use it to title one of the pages in their scrapbook. A nickname is one of the many things that you think you'll remember but if they outgrow it, you'll likely forget.

5. Look beyond the people and tangible items in your photographs. What do you see? What does this picture make you think about? Maybe you see an "Attitude" or you might be reminded of all your special "Memories" with this person. If you don't find the title or the topic you are looking for, try simply using that word or phrase as the title. ex.- ATTITUDE *or* MEMORIES.

6. If you are still at a loss for words, use the tip above but add a simple adjective or two in front of your topic.
ex.- My Favorite Toy *or* A Special Gift

2,001 Top Titles & Tips

Airplane
(see also Vacation)

Aim High
Up, Up, and Away
Take Flight
Flying High

Amusement Park

Joy Ride
A Land of Imagination
Hang On
Up and Down, Around and Around

Angel

Angels Watching Over Us
Shh...Angel Sleeping
This Is How An Angel Sleeps...
Grandparents are Angels in Disguise
Precious Angel
My Guardian Angel
I'm No Angel
Our Baby Angel
A Perfect Angel
Children are Angels with Crooked Halos

Animal
(see also specific animals)
Down on the Farm
Party Animal
God's Creatures
Petting Zoo

Anniversary
(see also Love)
Together Forever
Still Going Strong After All These Years
Then and Now
Through the Years
A Life of Love
Happy Yesterdays, Happier Tomorrows
Happily Married for 15 Years

Antiques
(see Heritage)

Ant
No Ifs, Ants, or Bugs About It
Ants in My Pants

Apple
The Apple of My Eye
Bushels of Fun
The Apple Doesn't Fall Far from the Tree
School Days
As American as Apple Pie

When Life Gives You Apples, Make
    Applesauce
A is for Apple
One Bad Apple in the Bunch
Sour Apples
Picking-N-Grinning
The Pick of the Crop

Archery
BULLSEYE
Right on Target
Sharpshooter
Straight as an Arrow

Armed Forces
(see Military)

Art
(see also Color/Coloring)
Look What I Did
A Work of Art
A Real Piece of Work
Beauty is in the Eye of the Beholder
Masterpiece
Imagination
The Next Picasso

Attitude

I'm in Charge Here
This Is How It's Gonna Be...
I'm the BOSS
COCKY
I'm Too Cute for Words
Big Shot
The Divine Divas
DIVA

Autumn

(see Fall)

Baby

(see also Boy, Child, and Girl)

New Life, New Love
Oh, Baby!
A Gift From Above
Our Bundle From Heaven
Our Perfect Angel
Our Baby Angel
Baby Me
Our New Arrival
A Labor of Love
A Star is Born
I Have Arrived
PERFECTION
Introducing the World's Most Beautiful
    Baby
It's a Boy!
It's a Girl!
The Love of Our Lives
You've Got the Cutest Little Baby Face
A Bundle of Joy
Lying in the Lap of Luxury
Great Things Come in Small Packages
Our Dream Come True
God's Greatest Gift
An Answered Prayer

Our Special Delivery
A Lullaby Moment
Ten Tiny Toes
A Button Nose, Cherry Lips and Ten Tiny
    Toes

Baking

FLOUR POWER
Cutie Pie
Let 'em Eat Cake
From the Kitchen of Rachel *(put your title on a die cut label or make a recipe card)*
I'll Have My Cake and Eat it Too
As American as Apple Pie
Sugar and Spice and Everything Nice
SWEETTOOTH
What's Cooking, Good Looking?

Ball

    (see also Sports and specific games)
Havin' a Ball
Play Ball!
ALL-STAR

Baptism

A Blessing
A Child of God
Our Child of God
Sunday's Child is Full of Grace

Barn
(see also Country and Animal)

Lil' Farmer
Lil' Farmer Mathew
Down on the Farm
Hay, There!
Having a Hay Day

Baseball
(see also Sports)

Lil' Slugger
Our Little Slugger
HOMERUN
Take Me Out to the Ball Game
ALL-STAR
All-Star in Training
Havin' a Ball
Play Ball
Major Leagues, Here I Come
Hit and Run
Seventh-Inning Stretch

Basketball
(see also Sports)

WHOOSH!
Nothing But Net
BIG SHOT
HOT SHOT

Laying Bricks
He Shoots! He Scores!
MVP
MVP in Training

Bathtime
(see also Bubblebath/Bubbles)
Luv the Tub
Squeaky Clean
Soap Opera
Rub a Dub in a Tub
Rub a Dub Dub Two Boys in a Tub
All Washed Up
Wet-n-Wild
Bathing Beauty
Did You Say "Bathtime" or "Playtime"?
SPLISH SPLASH

Beach
Beach Bum
The Prince and His Sand Castle
A Princess and Her Castle
Beach Babes
Beach Babies
The Beauty and the Beach
Happy as a Clam
Getting Wave Reviews
Catch a Wave
A Beautiful Day for the Beach
The Sands of Time

Feelin' Crabby
Down by the Sea Shore
Jewels of the Sea
A Seashell Search on the Seashore

Bear

The Bear Necessities
Someone Beary Special
Grin and Bear It
Please Bear With Me
I Love You Beary Much
Bear-y Special
Bear-ly 2 years old
As Cuddly as a Teddy Bear
G-R-O-W-L
GRIZZLY

Bee

Lil' Honeybee
The Queen Bee
Beecause I Love You
Beeing Cute
Cute as Can Bee
Catching a Buzz
Bee Sweet
Sweet as Honey
Hi, Honey!
Buzz Off!

Bicycle
(see also Firsts)

TRYcycle
If at First You Don't Succeed...
Try, Try Again
PEDDLER
Happy Trails
Practice Makes Perfect
Backyard Bike-a-thon
Have Some Balance in Your Life
Steady...Steady...
Trial and Error
Trail and Error
Hittin' the Trail
Trail Blazers
Steering Clear
Stop-N-Go

Birds
Birds of a Feather Flock Together
Feathered Friends
Flights of Fancy
Up, Up, and Away
Home Tweet Home
Lovebirds
Tweet Tweet
As Free as a Bird

The Early Bird Gets the Worm
As Light As A Feather
Backyard Beauty
Jailbird

Birthday

(see also Party or specific themes)
You're HOW OLD?
Aged to Perfection
An Oldie but Goodie
Make a Wish
SURPRISE!
I'll Have My Cake and Eat It Too
Let's Party!
With Age Comes Wisdom
It's the Big ONE
Bear-ly 2 Years Old
Still Young at Heart

Blocks

The Cute Kid on the Block
Block Party!

Boat

Row, Row, Row Your Boat
Anchors Away
Ahoy, Matey
Ships Ahoy
Sail Away

Book

(Try using the title and theme from a favorite book. Another suggestion: Title this page with a phrase your child uses when asking you to read.
ex. "Read Me, Mommy"

Bedtime Story
STORYTIME
An Open Book
An Open Book Opens Minds

Bowl

SuperBowl
Life is a BOWL of Cherries
You Bowl Me Over

Boxing
(see Fight/Fighting)

Boy/Boys
(see also Son)

Boys Will Be Boys
No Girls Allowed
It's a Guy Thing
Pure Boy
All Boy
The Boys of Summer
Bouncing Baby Boy

Oh, Boy!
Brotherly Love
Snakes and Snails and Puppy Dog Tails
Rough and Tumble

Boyfriend
(see also Date and Love)
My One and Only
CRUSH
Puppy Love
Boy Meets Girl
A True Romantic
Opposites Attract
Cute Couple
Beauty and the Beast
So Far, So Good

Boy Scouts
Scouts Honor
Always Prepared

Break-Up
New Beginnings
Love Hurts
Divorce Court
Out With the Old, In With the New
Letting Go
Give Me a Break
Time Heals
She Loves Me, She Loves Me Not

A Change of Heart
Good Riddance
C-YA!
See Ya' Around
A Good Man is Hard to Find

Brother
(see also Boys and Family)
My Brother, My Friend
Oh, Brother...
Friends from the Start
A Brother Understands
Brothers Since the Beginning, Friends 'Til
the End

Bubblebath/Bubbles
(see also Bath)
Bubble Trouble
A Bubbly Personality
Bubble-ing Over With Fun
Bubble-ing Over With Laughter
Double the Bubbles, Double the Fun
DOUBLY BOUBLY
Yummy Bubble Gummy
Blowing Bubbles
BUBBLE BUBBLE BUBBLE

Bug

CREEPY CRAWLY
BUG OFF
Cute as a Bug
As Snug as a Bug in a Rug
No Ifs, Ants, or Bugs About It
June Bugs
The Jitter Bug
Caught a Bug *(this is cute for a "sick" page)*
Bug Catcher
Cootie Bug
Quit Bugging Me
Love Bug
Bit by the Love Bug
Fashion Bug
SHUTTERBUG
Computer Bug

Bulldozer

DIG IT
Destruction Zone
Under Destruction
Caution: Boys at Play

Bus

The Wheels on the Bus Go 'Round and 'Round
Bus Boy

Butterfly

Butterfly Kisses
FLITTER FLITTER
Well, Flitter!
As Gentle as a Butterfly
Butterfly Beauty
Backyard Beauty

Cake

(see also Baking)

Let 'em Eat Cake
I'll Have My Cake and Eat It Too
SWEETTOOTH

Camera

Picture This
SMILE
Say "Cheese"
Strike A Pose
Everyday Moments
Picture Perfect
Priceless...
O.K., Take It
Hammin' It Up
Capture the Moment
Capture the Memories
Pretty as a Picture
Miles of Smiles
Freeze Frame
Superstar
I'm a Star!
A Picture is Worth a Thousand Words
Let's See What Develops
Shutterbug
Big Shot

Lights, Camera, Action!
Grin and Bear It
Ain't I Cute?
Show Us Those Pearly Whites

Camping
Happy Campers
S'More Good Times
Our Neck of the Woods
What Was That Noise?
Did You Hear That?
Under the Stars
The Great Outdoors
Roughin' It

Candy
(see also Chocolate)
So Much Candy, So Little Time
SWEETHEART
SWEETTOOTH
Sweets for a Sweetie
Sweet, Like Me
CANDYLAND
Give Me Some Sugar, Baby

Car
(see also Driving and Vacation)
A Classic
Vroom Vroom
Driving Us Crazy

Carousel
Up and Down, 'Round and 'Round
MERRY-Go-Round

Cat
Copy Cat
Cats Are People Too
Here Kitty, Kitty!
Scaredy Cat
PURRfect
M-E-O-W
Fluffy is the Cat's Meow
The Nine Lives of Fluffy
Fancy Feline
Look What the Cat Dragged In
Playful as a Kitten
Crazy Cat

Chalk
(see also Art and Color/Coloring)
CHALK TALK
Chalk One Up for Cody

Cheerleader
(Use a line from a popular or favorite chant. Even if it's one that you're so tired of hearing, it makes YOU want to scream, this could be the one that brings back the most memories in the future.)
Go! Fight! Win!
We've Got Spirit, Yes We Do...
Team Leaders
Short Skirts and Attitudes
Pom Pom Girls
Team Spirit

Cherry
Life is a Bowl of Cherries
Cheery Cherries
I Love You Cherry Much
I Love You With a Cherry On Top
I Cherryish You
Cherry Lips

Chicken
Slick Chick
One Sick Chick
Cock-a-Doodle-Doo
C-O-C-K-Y

Child/Children
(see also Baby, Boy, Girl, and Cute)
*(Look at the titles listed under "Camera".
These can be used for many general
photographs.)*
As Good as Gold
A Child is God's Greatest Gift
Kiddin' Around
Child's Play
The World's Best Kid
Kool Kid
Children Make the World a Happier Place
Our Pride and Joy
A Child of All Seasons
Children Put the Magic in Life
A Child Enjoys Life's Simple Pleasures
Everyday Moments are Cherished
    Moments
Children are Angels with Crooked Halos

Chocolate
(see also Candy)
Eat Now, Diet Later
Choca-holic
Spoil Yourself
INDULGE
A Basic Necessity of Life

Christening

A Blessing
A Child of God
Our Child of God
Sunday's Child is Full of Grace

Christmas

(see also Gifts and Santa Claus)
Our Little Elves
Santa's Helper
All Hearts Come Home for Christmas
I'll Be Home For Christmas
'Tis the Season for Love
Home for the Holidays
Children Put the Magic in Christmas
'Twas the Night Before Christmas
Our Christmas Angel
As Stuffed as the Christmas Stockings
TRADITION
Christmas Cousins
A Holly, Jolly Christmas
Naughty or Nice
Trimming the Tree
Joy to the World
Wish List
Jolly Holidays
So Many Toys, So Little Time
Toys, Toys, Everywhere

Church

Our Sunday Best
A Blessing
Have Faith
Count your Blessings
Sunday's Child is Full of Grace
A Day of Rest
A Day of Grace

Circle

My Circle of Friends
Round 'em Up

Circus

The Big Top
The Greatest Show on Earth
Lions, Tigers, and Bears...Oh, My!
Clowning Around

Clock
(see Time)

Clothing
(see Dress-up)

Clouds
(see also Heaven and Rain)
Every Cloud Has a Silver Lining
Our Bundle From Heaven

Clown
So Silly
Clownin' Around

College
(see also Graduation or School)
*(Title this page with your school's name,
initials, mascot, or motto)*
College Bound
My Dorm Away from Home
Dorm Sweet Dorm

Color/Coloring
(see also Art)
Color Me Silly
The Many Colors of Trista
A Colorful Personality
Color My World
Showing My True Colors
Pretty Scribbles
Scribble Scribble Scribble
Doodle-ing

Computer
World Wide Web
The Wild, Wild Web
NETWORKING
Little Computer Bug
Connecting...
You've Got Mail

Cooking
(see also Baking)
We're Cookin' Now
What's Cookin', Good Lookin'?
Look What's Cooking
The Kitchen is the Heart of the Home
What's for Dinner?
The Taste Test
Special Recipe
Secret Ingredients
The Best You've Ever Tasted

Cookout
Backyard Burgers
Backyard Bash
The Grill of Your Life
Get Fired Up
A Family Tradition

Country
(see also Barn)
The Heart of the Country
Howdy
Field of Dreams
Yee-Haw!
Down on the Farm

Cousin
(see also Family)

Kissing Cousins
Christmas Cousins
My Cousin, My Friend

Cow

Lil' Cowpoke
Udderly Adorable
Got Milk?
Milkin' It For All It's Worth
HOWDY!

Cowboy

Giddy Up!
Lil' Cowpoke
Howdy, Pardner
HOWDY!
Round 'em Up
WANTED
$10,000 REWARD
The Best in the West
Stick 'em Up!
The Wild, Wild West
Yee-Haw!

Crafts
(see also Sewing)
Handmade with Love
C-R-A-F-T-Y
A Gift from the Heart
Look What I Made

Crawling
(see also Firsts)
Look Out World, Here I Come!
Going, Going, Gone
I Think I Can, I Think I Can, I Can!
The Little Engine that Could
Practice Makes Perfect

Crocodile
The Crocodile Hunter
Crocodile Tears
See Ya' Later, Alligator
After while, Crocodile

Cruise
Bon Voyage
Shipping and Handling
Cruisin'
Ships Ahoy
My Ship Has Finally Come In

Crying
(see also Sad)
Cry Baby
Don't Cry, Baby
Crocodile Tears
For Cryin' Out Loud
Growing Pains

Cut
(see also Injury)
On the Cutting Edge
Cuttin' Up
Cut It Out

Cute
Cute as a Button
Just as Cute as I Can Be
Cute-N-Cuddly
Cutie Pie
Little Charmer
Prince Charming
Personality Plus
Absolutely Adorable
Too Cute For Words
You've Got the Cutest Lil' Baby Face
Cute Couple
Cute is My Middle Name
I Couldn't be More Lovable if I Tried

Daddy
(see also Father)

Dance
(see also Music)
Dance the Night Away
Two Left Feet
Twinkle Toes
SIDEKICKS *(appropriate for ballerinas)*
Tiny Dancer
The Baby Boogie
Dancin' to a Different Beat

Date
Cute Couple
Cherish the Moment
A Night on the Town
I Thought He'd Never Ask
How Did It Get So Late, So Early?
DREAMDATE

Daughter
(see also Baby, Child, and Girl)
A Daughter is a Reflection of Her
Mother's Heart
A Daughter is a Mother's Best Friend
Like Mother, Like Daughter

Death
(see also Memories)

Gone But Not Forgotten
An Angel Watches Over Us
Rest Peacefully
In Loving Memory
Keeping the Memory Alive
Unforgettable
I'll Love You Forever
We Miss You
Cherish the Memory
Sorrowful Day
Always Loved, Never Forgotten
My Guardian Angel

Dedication

A Blessing
Our Child of God
A Child of God
Sunday's Child is Full of Grace

Diet

Eat Now, Diet Later
Through Thick or Thin
Fit and Fabulous
Slim and Trim
Living Large
Think Thin
Light as a Feather

Dinosaur
DINOmite!

Dirty
(see also Mess/Messy)
A Little Dirt Never Hurt Anybody
This Little Piggy
Lil' Pig
YUCK!
Pig Sty
What's a Little Mud Between Two Friends?
Getting Down and Dirty

Divorce
(see Break-up)

Doctor
(see also Illness or Injury)
(Suggestion: "Diagnose" your subject. ex-Diagnosis:Touchmenotitis)
This Won't Hurt a Bit
This Hurts Me More Than it Hurts You
Say, "Ahhh"
Miracle Cure
FIRST AID
Nevermind, I'm Suddenly Feeling Better
Dr. SCARY
Nurse Starla
Dr. Trent

Diagnosis: Spoiledrottenitis
Diagnosis: Homesick
Diagnosis: Lovesick
A Clean Bill of Health
A Picture of Health
What's Up, Doc?
All Better

Dog
Snakes and Snails and Puppy Dog Tails...
Puppy Love
A Boy's Best Friend
Take a Bow-Wow
Hot Diggity-Dog!
Pampered Pooch
Dog Days of Summer
It's a Dog's Life
Doggone Adorable
Make No Bones About It...I'm Cute!
Puppy Play

Doll
(see also Baby)
All Dolled Up
Living Dolls

Dress-up
(see also Fairytale)
All Dressed Up - Where Can We Go?
All Dressed Up with No Place to Go
You've Got Style, Baby
All Dolled Up
Hot Stuff
Glamour Girl
Best Dressed
Accessorize, Accessorize, Accessorize
How Do I Look?
Lookin' Good
How Do You Like Me Now?

Driving
(see also Car and Wreck)
On the Road Again
Stop-N-Go
Begin Your Journey
Driving Me Crazy
Are We There Yet?
The Grand Prix
Speed Racer
Going the Extra Mile
How Much Longer?
Steering Clear
No Direction in Life

Two Wrong Turns Don't Make a Right
Along for the Ride
Hang On
The Ride of My Life

Drums
(see also Music)
Lil' Drummer Boy
BANG! CLASH! BANG!

Earth
(see World)

Easter
An Egg-stra Special Easter
Hoppy Easter
There's Nobunny Like You
He is Risen
Keep Your Eye on the Prize
The Thrill of the Hunt
The Hunt Is On
Everybunny Loves Me
Somebunny Special
Hopping Down the Bunny Trail
Hippity!Hoppity!Happy Easter!
Don't Put All Your Eggs In One Basket
Eggstatic!
An Egg-stra Fun Day
Egg-specially Cute

Eating
(see also MESSY)
Mmm!Mmm!Good!
YUMMY
All I Want to Do is Chew Chew Chew
MUNCHTIME
Eating Again?
The Princess and the Peas
Eat Now, Diet Later

I Love You Alunch
Let's Eat
Lunch Munch
Eat, Drink, and Be Merry

Eggs

An Egg-stra Big Mess
Don't Put All Your Eggs In One Basket
Egg-static
Egg-specially Cute

Engagement

(Use a quote from this special day)

YES
I said, "Yes"
I Thought You Would Never Ask
ENGAGED
Breathtaking
This Magic Moment
Always and Forever
Engaged at Last

Exercise

Eat Now, Exercise Later
Burnin' Calories
No Pain, No Gain
The Way I See it is...No Pain, No Pain
HUFF HUFF HUFF
...and Breathe, 2, 3, 4...
Feeling Fit
Fit and Firm
HARDBODY
Hardbody in Training
Feel the Burn
BUFF
Pumped Up
Huffin' and Puffin'
Be Strong
Firm, Fit, and Fabulous

Fairytale
(see also Dress-up)

Once Upon a Time...
As You Wish...
Her Majesty
The King and His Castle
Queen for a Day
Our Little Prince
Our Princess
My Knight in Shining Armor
The Royal Jester
ROYALTY
Hear Ye, Hear Ye...
Use Your Imagination
I Believe...
Daydream Believer
...Happily Ever After

Fall
(see also Pumpkin)

Harvest Time
Harvest Happiness
Pumpkin' Patch
Turning Over a New Leaf
On a Crisp Autumn Day...
The Cool Crisp Days of Autumn
Fall Into Fun
Piles of Fun
A Child of All Seasons
A Crisp Breeze and Crunchy Leaves

A Sign of the Season
It's Fall, Ya'll
Having a Hay Day
Hay, There!

Family

Family Matters
A Family Affair
The Ties that Bind the Family Together
All in the Family
A Family that Prays Together Stays
    Together
A Family that Plays Together Stays
    Together
One Big Happy Family
Family Portrait
Our Legacy
Remember Your Roots
LEAVE Your Mark
The Pell Legacy
GENERATIONS
We Begin and End With Family
Family Values
Obviously, Good Looks Run in the Family

Family Tree
(see Family, Heritage)

Farm
(see Barn and Country)

Father

My Hero
Like Father, Like Son
Like Daddy, Like Daughter
Daddy's Girl
Daddy's Little Helper

Father-in-Law

My Other Father
Father by Marriage
His Father, My Friend

Feet

Put Your Best Foot Forward
Kick Up Your Heels
There's Nothing More Sweet Than the
    Pitter Patter of Little Feet
Pitter Patter
Ten Tiny Toes
BAREFOOT
Barefoot and Fancy Free
Footloose and Fancy Free
2 Left Feet
Stinky Feet
You Knock My Socks Off
This Little Piggy...
The Agony of Defeet
Shoo!
Step-by-Step
Step by Tiny Step

Fight/Fighting

Down for the Count
A Real Knockout
Puttin' Up a Fight
Put 'em Up!
Keep Your Eye on the Prize
Rough and Tumble
Fight Night
A Fight 'Til the End

Fire

Jumping Out of the Frying Pan, Into the Fire
HOT HOT HOT
Up in Flames
Where's the Fire?
Don't Play With Fire
Hot Stuff
Where There's Smoke, There's Fire

Firsts

There's a First Time for Everything
Life is Full of Firsts
The First Time Around
I Think I Can, I Think I Can, I Can!
The Little Engine that Could
Look What I Can Do!
Practice Makes Perfect
I Did It!
I'll Do Anything Once

Fish/Fishing

The Catch of the Day
There's Something Fishy Going On Here
Fishing for Compliments
I'm a Keeper
Gone Fishin' (Again)
Look What I Caught

Flower
(see also Gardening)

Love in Bloom
Blooming Idiots
Friendship in Bloom
Memory is the Power to Gather Roses in
    Winter
Flower Power
Spring Has Sprung
Growing Like a Weed
A Rose By Any Other Name Smells Just
    As Sweet
Stop and Smell the Roses
April Showers Bring May Flowers
Backyard Beauty
An Annual Event
A Perennial Favorite
Sow Seeds of Kindness
He Loves Me, He Loves Me Not
Freshly Picked with You in Mind
Hand-painted by Angels

Football

(see also Sports)

*(Use a catch phrase from your favorite
team or game announcer.
ex-"It's Football Time in Tennessee!")*

Touchdown!

MVP

MVP in Training

Friend

Bestest Buddies

The Best of Friends, The Best of Times

2 Peas In A Pod

Two of a Kind

Friendship in Bloom

My Circle of Friends, Let It Never Be
    Broken

Friends 'Til the End

Two's Company

Three's Company

Friends Forever

Friends Through Thick or Thin

Me and My Shadow

Friends in Sunshine and in Shade

Sidekicks

Love One Another

Gossip Gossip Gossip

Frog

Ribbit Ribbit
Don't Worry, Be Hoppy
It Ain't Easy Being Green
Kiss Me...
I May Be A Prince, You Never Know
Is This Leap Year?
Feelin' Froggy? Jump!

Gambling
(see also Money)
Life's a Gamble
Poker Face
Slot Machine Queen
Gotta Know When to Hold 'Em
Ante Up!
I'll Betcha
Let's Make a Deal
The Luck of the Draw
All Bets Are Off

Gardening
(see also Flower)
Harvest Love
How Does Your Garden Grow
Sow Seeds of Kindness
Our Little Sprout
The Pick of the Crop
Pickin' and Grinnin'
Gettin' Down and Dirty

Gifts
Just What I've Always Wanted
The Perfect Gift
The Past and the Presents
Presents, Presents Everywhere
THANK YOU
Just For You

You REALLY Shouldn't Have
A Gift From the Heart
Big Things Come in Small Packages
Children are God's Greatest Gift

Girl/Girls
(see also Daughter)
Girls Just Want to Have Fun
Sugar and Spice and Everything Nice...
SASSY
It's a Girl Thing
Girls Rule!
DIVA
The Divine Divas
Girl Talk
Girl Power
Princess
Our Little Princess
Glamour Girls
Girl's Night Out
Little Dolls
You Go Girl!
Daddy's Girl
Pure Girl

Girlfriend
(see also Date and Love)
My One and Only
CRUSH
Puppy Love
A True Romantic
Beauty and the Beast
Opposites Attract
Boy Meets Girl
So Far, So Good

Girl Scouts
Scouts Honor
Be Prepared
Make New Friends

Glasses
SPECtacular
Stay Focused
Set Your Sights High

Golf
FORE!
A Hole in Four
TEErific
The Swinger

Graduation

I Did It!
Congrats Grad!
College Bound
CONGRATULATIONS
FINALLY
Now I Can Get a Real Job
The Future Looks Bright
Thanks Mom and Dad!
Edgicated
Now What?
The Graduate
The Scholar
Follow Your Dreams
If You Can Dream It, You Can Be It
Reach For the Stars
Believe in Yourself
Beginning a New Journey
I Thought This Day Would Never Come
Opportunity Knocks
All Grown Up

Grandchildren

(see also Baby and Child/Children)
They Don't Call 'Em Grand For Nothing
Grandchildren Make Life Grand
Grandchildren Put the Magic Back in Life
My Grandchildren are the Grandest of
     Them All

Grandfather

(see also Grandparents)

My Hero

Call Grandpa: 1-800-I-Want-It

My Grandpa is the Grandest of Them All

A Day with Grandpa is a Priceless Day

Priceless Wisdom

Grandmother

(see also Grandparents)

Over the River and Through the Woods...

To Grandmother's House We Go

When a Child is Born, So Is A
     Grandmother   *-Italian proverb*

Matriarch

The Lap of Luxury

A Timeless Beauty

Call Grandma: 1-800-I-Want-It

Golden Girl

A Woman of Wisdom

Priceless Wisdom

My Grandma is the Grandest of Them All

A Day in Grandma's Kitchen is a
Priceless Day

Snacks Taste Better at Grandma's House

Grandparents

With Age Comes Wisdom
Grandparents are Angels in Disguise
They Don't Call 'Em Grand For Nothing
Grandparents Make Life Grand

Grow/Growing

Growing by Leaps and Bounds
Growing Like a Weed
Measuring Up
When I Grow Up
So Big
Growing, Growing, Grown
Not a Baby Anymore
Growing Pains
All Grown Up

Gymnastics

TUMBLIN'
SHOWOFF
It's All in the Execution
It's All in the Landing
Have Balance in Your Life
I'd Bend Over Backwards for You
Flipped Out

Hair

Hair Today, Gone Tomorrow
Buzzzz Cut *(use Bee paper, stickers, or die cuts)*
Curl Crazy
Bald is Beautiful
Bad Hair Day
Just a Trim, Please
My 1st Haircut
The Mane Event
Knot Head
Big Hairy Deal
Rapunzel, Rapunzel
GOLDILOCKS
CURLYLOCKS
Snip, Snip, Snip
Simply to DYE for
On the Cutting Edge
Bed Head
Peach Fuzz
Knotty But Nice

Halloween

(Using large letters, spell out Halloween across your page. Use a Jack-O-Lantern in place of the "O". The Jack-O-Lantern will be in the center of your page.)
So Much Candy, So Little Time
CANDYLAND
BOO!

TRICK or TREAT
WICKED
BOOtiful!
Fright Night
Witch You Were Here
A Bewitching Evening
Casting a Spell
Scaredy Cat

Hand
(Stamp your child's handprint on each side of the title to give the appearance that he/she is holding the title)
HANDle With Care
Look Mom, No Hands!
Loving Hands
I'm a Real Handful
A Hands Down Favorite
So HANDsome
Gimme a Hand, Please
Hold On
Caught Red-Handed

Handmade
(See Art, Baking, Crafts, and Sewing)

Hanukkah
Shining Bright

Happy

On Top of the World
Don't Worry, Be Happy
Happy as a Clam
Happy Days
Good Times

Harvest

(see Fall, Gardening, Pumpkins)

Hat

Hats Off to You
The Mad Hatter

Heart

(see also Love)

Heart to Heart
A Work of Heart
My Heart and Soul
The Heart of the Country
Be Still My Heart
A Gift from the Heart
Follow Your Heart
Home is Where the Heart Is
I Love You With All My Heart

Heaven

A Gift from Above
Heaven Sent
Our Bundle from Heaven
A Blessing
A Match Made in Heaven
Heaven on Earth

Heritage

(see also Family and Memories)
A Grandma is an Antique Little Girl
A Classic
Yesteryear
An Oldie but Goodie
Beauty From the Past
From Past to Present
From Days Gone By
Making History
Then and Now
A Timeless Treasure
Nostalgia
It All Starts and Ends With Family
Step Back in Time

Hiking

Happy Trails
Take A Hike
A Walk On the Wild Side
Welcome to Our Neck of the Woods
Trail of Good Times

Trail and Error
Headed Down the Wrong Path
Trail Blazers
Nature Hike
Hike It Up
Hittin' the Trail

Hockey
(see also Sports)

He Shoots! He Scores!
GOAL!
SCORE!
Cold as Ice
Too Cool

Home/House
(see also Remodeling)

There's No Place Like Home
Home Is Where The Heart Is
Love Makes a House a Home
Fixer Upper
Our Dream House
We've Moved
New Address, New Attitude
Cozy and Charming
The American Dream
House + Love = Home
Our Mansion
Our Lil' Cottage

Room to Breathe
Great Things Come in Small Packages
Home Sweet Home
Home Sweet Apartment

Horse

Horse Play
Horsin' Around
Straight from the Horse's Mouth
Giddyup
Round 'Em Up
Why the Long Face?
The Mane Event

Hug

Bear Hug
Cuddle Buddies
Cute-N-Cuddly
Cheek to Cheek
XOXOXO
As Cuddly as a Teddy Bear
Cuddles and Kisses
Love One Another
Embrace Life
A Special Hug for You, From Me

Hunting

Daddy's Little Dear
Huntin' Buddies
Big Shot
On the Hunt
The Buck Stops Here
Hunting Season
BULLSEYE!
Sharpshooter

Ice Cream

Ice Cream Weather
It Takes a Lickin'
SWEET
Sweets for the Sweeties
Licking the Heat
Hey, Good Lickin'
A Taste of Summer

Illness
(see also Doctor)

Sick Chick
Laughter is the Best Medicine
Caught a Bug
Road to Recovery
Lovesick
Life is Fragile. Handle With Prayer.
In Sickness and In Health...
Prescription: Tender Loving Care
Feeling Under the Weather
Love Conquers All
A Picture of Health
Moanin' and Groanin'
Oh, My Aching....

Independence Day

All American
All American Kid
A Festive Fourth
God Bless America

Happy Birthday, America
The Land That I Love

Injury

OUCH!
OOPS!
Life is Fragile. Handle With Care.
Trial and Error
My Boo-Boo
Mommy Cried More Than Me
The Road To Recovery
All Stitched Up
You Keep Me In Stitches
Prescription: Tender Loving Care
The CASTing Couch
First Aid
The Agony of DeFEET
Moanin' and Groanin'
Oh, My Aching...
Time Heals All Wounds
Gimme a Break
EMERGENCY

Inspirational

Live in the Moment
Reach for the Stars
I Think I Can, I Think I Can, I Can!
Stop and Smell the Roses
Notice the Little Things
Cherish the Moment

Job
(see Money and Work)

Jumping

A Leap of Faith
By Leaps and Bounds
Growing by Leaps and Bounds
Popping Up All Over the Place
Jumping Out of the Frying Pan, Into the
    Fire
Feeling Froggy? Jump!
Jump for Joy
A Hop, Skip, and Jump Away
Bouncing Baby Boy
Don't Worry, Be Hoppy
Is This Leap Year?

Kindergarten
(see also School)
Mommy Cried, I Played
Making New Friends

Kiss

Butterfly Kisses
A Kiss for Luck
S.W.A.K.
HOTLIPS
The Kiss of Death
Turn the Other Cheek
Ooh! Cooties!
Kiss Me Baby
Cute Couple
Tanner and Jacquelyn, sitting in a tree,
    K-I-S-S-I-N-G
Planting Twolips
Kissing Cousins
Give Me Some Sugar, Baby
Hello, Sweetlips!
As Sweet as Sugar
A Kiss is Just a Kiss
XOXOXO
Hugs and Kisses
SMOOCHING
Simply Irresistible
Love One Another
Cuddle and Kisses

Kite

Flying High
Up, Up, and Away
High in the Sky
Aim High
Go Fly a Kite
If at First You Don't Succeed, Try, Try
    Again

Knife

(see Cut)

Knot

Knotty But Nice
All Tied Up at the Moment
The Ties That Bind
I Think Knot
Knot Me
Knot Head

Laugh/Laughing/Laughter
Giggle Giggle Giggle
Tickled Pink
Laughter is the Best Medicine

Love
(Title this page with a line from
"your song".)
Love is in the Air
Love in Bloom
Young Love
Puppy Love
My Best Friend, My True Love
The Love Bug
Love Hurts
A Life of Love
Always and Forever
My Love
Ain't Love Grand?
Lovebirds
Lovesick
The Love of My Life
Love Letters
A Match Made in Heaven
World's Happiest Couple
I'll Love You Forever
Unconditional Love
Forever and Ever
Everlasting Love
My Knight in Shining Armor

I Love You With All My Heart
Love Makes Life Complete
My One and Only
True Love
Love Conquers All
He Loves Me, He Loves Me Not
How Do I Love Thee? Let Me Count the
    Ways...

Make-believe
(see Cowboy, Fairytale, or Pirate)

Memories
Memory Lane
Memories in the Making
Memory is the Power to Gather Roses in
  Winter
Memories for a Lifetime
Keeping the Memory Alive
Magical Memories
Remember When...
These are the Times to Remember
The Way It Was
Cherished Days
Priceless...
For Old Times Sake
Gone But Not Forgotten
The Good Ol' Days
I Remember When...
Where Did the Time Go?
Through the Years
Seems Like Yesterday
Treasured Thoughts
Everyday Moments Become Cherished
  Memories

Men

It Must Be a Guy Thing
Manly Man
A Jack-of-All-Trades
A Good Man is Hard to Find

Mess/Messy
(see also Dirty)

What a Mess
Trashed
Look What I Did
I'm a Mess
Could Somebody Bring Me a Mop?
Have You Ever Seen Such a Mess?
Uh-Oh!
Oops!

Military

Ready, Willing, and Able *(U.S. ARMY)*
Wings of Victory *(U.S. Air Force)*
Above and Beyond *(U.S. Air Force)*
Proud to Serve *(U.S. Navy)*
Our Hero
Military Man
Stand at Ease
The Unsung Hero
Rank and File
Above and Beyond the Call of Duty

Milk

MOOre Milk, Please
Milk Mustache
Milkin' it for All it's Worth
Milk Does a Body Good
Got Milk?
Udderly Delicious
Udderly Adorable

Model

Role Model

Money

Show Me the Money
$$$$$
Cha-Ching!
MOOLAH
Ooh la la! Moolah!
Right on the Money
Rolling in the Dough
I'm Rich!
Who Wants To Be A Millionaire?
Big Spender
Deep in Debt
Cash Flow
Penny Pincher
I Owe! I Owe! Off to Work I Go!
For Richer, For Poorer
The Buck Stops Here
The Lap of Luxury

Monkey

Going Bananas
Monkey on My Back
Hear No Evil, See No Evil
Monkey Business
Monkey-ing Around
Monkey See, Monkey Do

Moon

(see also Sleep)
The Man in the Moon
Goodnight

Mother

Like Mother, Like Daughter
Mommy and Me
All that I am or Hope to be, I Owe to My
    Mother *-Abraham Lincoln*
Every Mother is a Working Woman
Unconditional Love
Always Caring, Always Giving, Always
    Loved
A Mother's Touch
Mother's Loving Ways
A Mom of All Trades
A Mother's Work is Never Done
A Mother is a Girl's Best Friend
The Best Friend a Daughter Could Ever
    Have

Mother-in-Law

My Other Mother
Mother by Marriage
His Mother, My Friend

Motorcycle

Born to be Wild

Music

I've Got Rhythm
Feel the Rhythm
Encore! Encore!
Let the Music Play
Rock-N-Roll
A Little Bit Country, A Little Bit
    Rock-N-Roll
A Band of Gold
Sing Along
Music to My Ears
Practice Makes Perfect
Practice, Practice, Practice

Newspaper

Extra! Extra!
News Flash
Front Page News
Making News
Have You Heard the Good News?

New Year
(see also Party)
Out With the Old, In With the New
The Future Looks Bright
CELEBRATION
Celebrate Good Times
WELCOME 2001
GOODBYE 2000
I Resolve to...
Good Times are Here to Stay
A Big End to a Big Year
A Great Start for a Great Year to Come

Noah's Ark

Two by Two
Flooded With Blessings
All Aboard!

Nude

Naked Again
Is it Cold in Here or Is it Just Me?
The Nude Kid on the Block
Are Ya' Naked?
As Free as a Bird
SASSY
Bare Bottom
Centerfold Material
BAREly 2 years old
BAREly covered

Odor

SCENTsational
Lil' Stinker
Shoo!

Park
(see also Picnic, Slide, and Swing)
A Day at the Park
A Walk in the Park

Party
Let's Party
It's Party Time
The More the Merrier
How Did It Get So Late, So Early?
You're Invited
It's My Party and I'll Cry If I Want To
The Life of the Party
In High Spirits
Party Girl
Party Animal
Raise the Roof
Eat, Drink, and be Merry

Passover
Shining Bright

Peach
Peach Fuzz
Peachy Keen
Life's Just Peachy
What a Peach

Pet
(see also specific animals)
Our Zoo
Petting Zoo

Piano
(see also Music)
Baby Grand
Baby, I'm Grand
Baby, Ain't Life Grand
Practice Makes Perfect
RECITAL

Picnic
Picnic in the Park
A Taste of Summer
Life is a Picnic
Life's No Picnic
No Ifs, Ants, or Bugs About It

Pie
(see also Baking)
Cutie Pie
Sweetie Pie
SWEETTOOTH
Georgey Porgy Pudding Pie

Pig

This Little Piggy...
OINK OINK OINK
Porky
When Pigs Fly...
Pig Sty

Pirate

Hidden Treasures
Our Little Treasure
Walk the Plank
Captain Colt
Aye, Aye, Captain

Photography
(see Camera)

Play
(see also Star)
Hollywood, Here I Come
All the World's a Stage
Theater of Dreams
Center Stage
Break a Leg
There's No Business Like Show Business
Child's Play
Lights, Camera, Action!

Pool
(see Swimming)

Pose
(see Camera)

Prom
(The prom's theme song will probably be a good title for this layout)
Memories in the Making
A Night to Remember
Dancing the Night Away
Oh, What a Night
Dream Date
Cute Couple

Pumpkin
Lil' Pumpkin
Pumpkin Patch
Pickin' Pumpkins
Picking and Grinning
Carvin' Time
A Sign of the Season
The Pick of the Crop

Puppy
(see Dog)

Puzzle
The Missing Link
Hmm, Puzzle-ing
It's a Puzzle to Me, Too
Falling to Pieces

Rabbit
There's No Bunny Like You
Somebunny Special
Hopping Down the Bunny Trail
Hippity!Hoppity!Happy!
Somebunny Loves Me

Race/Racing
(see also Driving)
Speed Racer
Pit Stop
Gentlemen, Start Your Engines
Race Day
From Start to Finish
The Grand Prix

Rafting
WHITEWATER
Riding the Rapids
Man Overboard
Row, Row, Row Your Raft
A Whitewater Misadventure

Rain
Our Rainy Day Sunshine
Singing in the Rain
A Damp Dark Day
Look on the Bright Side
Showered With Love
Sprinkles On Top

Sprinkled With Love
Rainy Day Fun
Raindrops Keep Fallin' On My Head
Sprinkle Sprinkle Sprinkle
Feeling Under the Weather
Rain, Rain, Go Away, Come Again
Another Day
April Showers Bring May Flowers
Rain, Rain, Go Away
It's Raining It's Pouring
DOWNPOUR
Raining Cats and Dogs
When It Rains, It Pours
Showers Bring Flowers

Rainbow
Look on the Bright Side...
Rainy Day Reward
Color My World
Color Me Silly
A Colorful Personality
Somewhere Over the Rainbow
Better than a Pot of Gold
Our Little Leprechaun
The Many Colors of Talisa
Show Your True Colors
Chasing Rainbows

Remodeling
(see also Tools)
A Work in Progress
Rome Wasn't Built in a Day
Raise the Roof
Room for Improvement
Fixer Upper
Room to Breathe
From Start to Finish
What a Difference

Retirement
FINALLY!
Now What?
I Thought This Day Would Never Come
What Will They Ever Do Without Me?
I'm Outta Here!
Do What You Like, Like What You Do
Time for a Little R&R
Professional Tourist
Well Deserved

Reunion
How Long Has It Been?
It's Been Too Long
Reunited After All These Years
Where Have You Been All My Life?
Together At Last
I've Missed You

Rock

A Milestone
Rock-N-Roll
Rock Bottom
Boulder and Beautiful
Rock-A-Bye Baby
Between a Rock and a Hard Place

Rocking Chair/ Horse

Rockin' and Rollin'
We're Rocking Now!
A Rocking Good Time

Rolling Over

(see also Firsts)
Over and Over Again
Flipped Out
Rolling Through Life
Roll-y Poll-y
Rock-n-ROLL
Just Roll with it, Baby

Rubberducky

Squeaky Clean
Quack! Quack! Quack!

Run/Running

Ready, Set, GO!
Going, Going, Gone
Goin' Places
Runnin' Wild
Road Runner
From Start to Finish
It Runs in the Family

Sad
(see also Crying)
Why the Long Face?
Soooo Sad
Sorrowful Day
Don't Worry, Be Happy

Santa Claus
(Include a list of what your child asked for
this year and what was received)
Dear Santa,
Santa and Me
Naughty or Nice?
A Jolly Old Soul
Jolly Little Souls
Cheeks Like Cherries
Do You Believe?
HO HO HO
Dear Santa, I've Been Good
Santa's Helper
Nevermind!
HO HO NO!
Our Little Elves
A Holly, Jolly Christmas
Our 1st Meeting
The Bearded Stranger
Jolly Holidays

Scare

BOO!
Did You Hear That?
What Was That?
Scaredy Cat
Hold Me

School

*(Title this layout with the school's name,
initials, mascot, or motto. Don't take for
granted that future generations will know
what school your subject went to.
Another suggestion:
Substitute the more common
"A is for Apple" with any letter and
word that is appropriate for your layout
ex.- D is for Dylan or L is for Lovin' School)*
School Spirit
School Days
School Daze
Back 2 School
My Favorite Subject
When is Recess?
When is Lunch?
Making the Grade
ABC's and 123's
S is for School
Making Progress
Future Honor Student
Honor Student in Training

Genius in Training
Star Student
Head of the Class
All Grown Up
Getting Edgicated

Scissors
(see Cut)

Scrapbooking
(see also Sticker)
Good 'til the Last Crop
Crop Everything
A Scrappin' Good Time
Saving Memories, Making New Ones
Saving Memories, Making Friends
Crop 'til You Drop
SCRAPAHOLICS
Just Call Me "Scrappy"
Made With Love
Capture the Memories
On the Cutting Edge
Ready! Set! CROP!
Cuttin' Up
For Generations to Come...

Sewing
(see also Crafts)
Sew Much Fabric, Sew Little Time
Cute as a Button
Sew Adorable
Sew Much Fun
Cut From the Same Cloth
A Stitch in Time...
You Keep Me in Stitches
I See a Pattern Here
Sew What!

Shine
Dazzling
All that Glitters is Not Gold
Look on the Bright Side

Shoe
(see also Feet)
My Heart and Sole
Shoo!
Kick Up Your Heels
Put Yourself in My Shoes
Put Your Best Foot Forward

Shopping
Born to Shop
Shopping is in Our Genes
We Came, We Shopped, We Conquered
Shop-a-holic

Let's Make a Deal
Shop 'til You Drop
Shopping Spree
Spending Spree
When Ya' Gotta Have It, Ya' Just Gotta
     Have It

Sick
(see Illness)

Sister
(see also Girl and Family)
My Sister, My Friend
Sisters Since the Beginning, Friends 'Til
     the End
Sister, Sister
A Sister Understands

Skate
Skate into Winter
Gliding Through Life
Glidin' Along
Rollin' Along
Just Roll with it, Baby
Skating on Thin Ice
Roller Derby
Slippin' and Slidin'

Skateboard
Glidin' Through Life
Gliding Along
Freestyling

Skiing
Hittin' the Slopes
It's All Downhill from Here
Hopping Down the Bunny Slope
Snow Bunny
Winter Wonderland
Water Whimsy
Just Gliding Through
Skiing Through Life
On a Downhill Slide

Sleep
Now I Lay Me Down To Sleep
Zzzzz
Recharging
Nite Nite
Shh...Angel Sleeping
This Is How An Angel Sleeps
A Lullabye Moment
Counting Sheep
It's Raining, It's Pouring, the Old Man is
    Snoring
Sweet Dreams
Sleepy Head
Early to Bed, Early to Rise

Follow Your Dreams
Sleeping In
Bed Head
All is Calm
As Snug as a Bug in a Rug
Life is but a Dream
May All Your Dreams Come True

Slide

Slip Slidin' Away
Slide Into Summer
Sliding Through Life
On a Downhill Slide

Smile

(see Camera)

Snake

Sssssssnakes
Here's the Sssssssssstory....
Snakes and Snails and Puppy Dog Tails

Snow

(see also Winter)
Our Little Eskimos
Snow Much Fun
Snow Angel
Snow Baby
Snow Day
B-L-I-Z-Z-A-R-D

Let it Snow, Let it Snow, Let it Snow
A Sign of the Season
BUNDLED
Snow Bunnies
No Two are Alike
FROSTY
The Snowball Champion
The 1999 Snowball Fighting
Championship

Soccer

SCORE
GOAL
I Get a Kick Out of You
Gettin' Our Kicks

Socks

Shoo!
Sock It To Me
You Knock My Socks Off
Kick Up Your Heels

Son

(see also Baby, Boy, and Child)
The Son that Brightens My Day
Our Little Sonshine
Like Father, Like Son

Spider

Itsy Bitsy Spider
CREEPY CRAWLY
Oh, What a Tangled Web We Weave...

Sports

(see specific sports also)
ALLSTAR
My Little All-star
Go! Fight! Win!
The Sports Page
Havin' A Ball
Team Spirit
Team Player
MVP
We're #1
Practice Makes Perfect
Practice, Practice, Practice
Sore Losers
Be A Winner
It's Not Whether You Win or Lose...
We'll Get 'Em Next Time
V-I-C-T-O-R-Y
The Champs

Spring

Spring Has Sprung
Spring to Life
Spring Fever
Spring Cleaning Time

Spring Fling
Love in Bloom
Swing Into Spring
April Showers Bring May Flowers
Spring Cleaning

Star

My Little All-Star
Twinkle Twinkle
A Shining Star
SUPERSTAR
I'm a Star!
Star Power
A Star is Born
Make a Wish...
When You Wish Upon a Star...
Reach for the Stars
A Star Performance
The Star of the Show

Sticker

Stick to What You Know
I'm Stuck on You
Stick 'em Up
A Sticky Situation
S-T-I-C-K-Y

St. Patrick's Day

Our Little Leprechaun
Lil' Leprechaun
The Luck of the Irish
Dance a Jig
Better Than a Pot of Gold
PINCHED

Strawberry

A Berry Special Boy
Strawberry Jam
A Strawberry Blonde

Stroller

Strollin' Along
I'm Outta Here!
Let's Get Out of Here
CRUISIN'

Summer

(see also Sun)

Lazy Summer Days
Hot Summer Days
Summer Fun
Barefoot and Fancy Free
HOT HOT HOT
Boys of Summer
Summer Lovin' Girls

Sun-Kissed
Too Cool to be Hot
Some Like it Hot
The Dog Days of Summer

Sun
You Light Up My Life
You Are My Sunshine
Fun in the Sun
Mr. Sun, Shine On Me
The Light of My Life
Friends in Sunshine and in Shade
Look on the Bright Side

Sunbathing/Sunburn
Soakin' Up Some Rays
Bathing Beauties
Sun-Kissed
Sunny Side Up
Itsy Bitsy Teenie Weenie Bikini
Bikini Babe
FRIED
Feel the Burn
HOT! HOT! HOT!
OUCH
SIZZLE
Too Hot to Handle
Well-Done
BAKING

Sunset

Serenity
Breathtaking
Blaze on the Horizon

Surfing

Body Surfing
Hangin' On for Dear Life
Hangin' Ten
Getting Wave Reviews
Whoa!
Surf's Up
Catch a Wave

Swimming

Dive In
Itsy Bitsy Teenie Weenie Bikini
Bikini Babe
Little Mermaid
Staying Cool in the Pool
SPLASH!
A Splashin' Good Time
Makin' Waves
Man Overboard
Wet 'N' Wild

Swing

Just-a-Swinging
Higher! Higher!
Up, Up and Away
Look at Me
Swing into Spring
Swing into Summer
Set Your Sights High
Rock-a-Bye Baby
Swing By Sometimes

Talking
(see also Firsts)
From the Mouths of Babes...
From the Mouths of Babes Comes Truth
Motor Mouth
The Mouth of the South
Gossip, Gossip, Gossip
Let's Talk About It
Say What?
Goo Goo DA DA *(Substitute your child's First words)*

Teacher/Teaching
Teachers Touch Tomorrow
Teaching is a Work of Heart
In Teaching Others, We Teach Ourselves
-proverb

Teenager
(Title this layout with a slang word or phrase that your teenager uses often)
WHATEVER
Hangin' Out

Teeth

(If your child has lost a tooth, use a quote about loosing the tooth or something said about the Toothfairy.
ex.- All I Got Was A Dollar!)

Tooth or Dare
Sweet Tooth
Toothless in Seattle
Pickin' and Grinnin'
Show Us Those Pearly Whites

Telephone

HELLO?
RING RING RING
Say What?
Let's Talk About It
Gossip Gossip Gossip
What Did We Do Before Call Waiting?

Thanksgiving

THANKS
A Time for Thanks
Turkey Time
A Thanksgiving Feast
Blessed Are We
Harvest of Happiness
As Stuffed as a Thanksgiving Turkey
STUFFED
Howdy Pilgrim
An Abundance of Blessings

Time

(Put clock hands inside the o's in your title or use clock hands in place of i's. Also, this could be a good place to do a timeline layout, showing the progression of a subject or event over a period of time)

Where Did the Time Go?
The Passage of Time
Time Lapse
Time-Out
Wait and See
Well Worth the Wait
The Sands of Time
Take Your Time
How Did It Get So Late, So Early?
Time Flies When You're Having Fun
If We Could Freeze Time...
A Timeless Beauty
Then and Now
Travel Back in Time
Time Heals All Wounds
Perfect Timing
Father Time
Wait a Minute

Toilet/Toilet Training

Who Needs Diapers? Not Me!
I'm a Big Boy Now
...In Training
A King and His Throne
When Ya' Gotta Go, Ya' Gotta Go
It's My Potty and I'll Cry If I Want To
Oops

Tongue

Tongue Twister
Hey, Good Lickin'
It Takes a Lickin'

Tools

A Jack-of-All-Trades
Tool Time
HANDYMAN
If You Build It, They Will Come
Under Construction
Under Destruction
Caution: Men at Work
Caution: Men at Play
Lil' Helper
Daddy's Big Helper
A Work in Progress
Rome Wasn't Built in a Day
Fixer Upper

Toys

(Does your child have a special name for his favorite toy? ex.- My Choo-Choo Also, try looking up more specific toys such as baby dolls, blocks, or bulldozer)

Toys, Toys Everywhere
You Can Never Have Too Many Toys
Look What I've Got
Just a Few of My Favorite Things
I'm Bored
So Many Toys, So Little Time

Tradition

A Time-honored Tradition
Family Tradition
An Annual Event
Same Time, Same Place, Different Year

Train

I Think I Can, I Think I Can, I Can!
(This is cute for a child doing something for the first time, such as learning to walk.)
Choo!Choo!
Chew!Chew!
The Little Engine that Could
Imagination Station
Welcome Aboard

Tree

Leave Your Mark
Turning Over a New Leaf

Treehouse

No Boys Allowed
No Girls Allowed
Home Away From Home
Home Sweet Wooden Home
Home Sweet Treehouse

Triplets

Triple Trouble
Three's Company
Three's a Crowd
Three of a Kind
Like 3 Peas in a Pod
Copy Cats
Split Personalities

Trouble

Caught in the Act
Caught Red-Handed
Here Comes Trouble
Who Me?
Trouble is My Middle Name
The Scene of the Crime
The Devil Made Me Do It
Oops
Is This Legal?

Hang Your Troubles Out To Dry
I Didn't Do It
The Usual Suspect
Problem Child
I'm a Real Handful
On the Wrong Side of the Law
Troublemaker

Twins

Double Trouble
Two's Company
Two of a Kind
Seeing Double
Like 2 Peas in a Pod
Copy Cats
Split Personality
Double Exposure

Ultrasound

(see also Baby)

Already Adorable
Here I Am!
Look Out World, Here I Come

Vacation

(see also Driving or Airplane)

Road Trip
On the Road Again
PARADISE
Our Paradise
Our Escape
The Great Escape
No Direction in Life
Going the Extra Mile
Are We There Yet?
How Much Longer?
Family Time
Family Retreat
A Mountain Retreat
Goin' Places
Rest and Relaxation
Miles of Smiles
The Time of Our Lives
Wish You Were Here
World Travelers
TOURISTS
Professional Tourists
Getting There is Half the Fun

Northern Exposure
Up North
Southern Charm
Southern Hospitality
Begin Your Journey

Valentine's Day
(Title this page with a phrase from a special Valentine you received. Include the card on the page if there is room.)
Happy Love Day
Be Mine
Be My Valentine
A Day for Love
Thanks Cupid!
My Favorite Valentine
My Funny Valentine

Volleyball
(see also Sports)
SPIKE!
Bump, Set, Spike!
ROTATE

Volunteer
A Labor of Love
Changing Lives
Do What You Like, Like What You Do
Making the World a Better Place
Touching Lives

Waiting
(see Time)

Walk/Walking
(see also Firsts)

First Steps
Look Mom! No Hands!
Ready, Set, Walk!
Goin' Places
STROLLIN'
Take a Stroll
Step-by-Step
Step by Tiny Step
Going, Going, GONE
Look Out World, Here I Come
Put Your Best Foot Forward

Watermelon

A Taste of Summer

Wedding
(see also Love)

I Do
Just Married
Happily Ever After
Always and Forever
A Dream Come True
Breathtaking Beauty
FOREVER

Winter
(see also Snow)

Winter Wonderland
Brrrrr!!!
Too Cool
If We Could Freeze Time...
Cold Days, Warm Hearts
Warmest Wishes
A Child of All Seasons

Work

I Owe! I Owe! Off to Work I Go
Waiting for the Weekend
A Labor of Love
Every Mother is a Working Woman
Working Together
Do What You Like, Like What You Do
T.G.I.F.
My Associates, My Friends
Opportunity Knocks
Business as Usual
A Hard Day's Work
It's All in a Day's Work
Another Day, Another Dollar
All Work, No Play

World

What Goes Around, Comes Around
On Top of the World
It's a Small World After All
Joy to the World
Making the World a Better Place
Children Make the World a Magical Place
World's Happiest Couple
World's Best Kid
As the World Turns

Worm

WIGGLE WIGGLE WIGGLE
The Early Bird Gets the Worm
Squirmy Worm

Wreck

(see also Driving)

Just Call Me Crash
Oops
A Nervous Wreck

Wrestling

World's Wackiest Friends
Show No Mercy
Take Down
PINNED
Rough and Tumble

Yell/Yelling

Ahhhhhh!!!
The Call of the Wild
Shout it from the Rooftops
I Scream, You Scream, We All Scream

Zoo

Lions, Tigers, and Bears...Oh, My!
Do the Zoo
Our Trip to the Zoo
Feedin' Time at the Zoo
Do Not Feed the Animals
Ever Feel Caged?
What a Zoo
WILDLIFE
The Call of the Wild
It's a Jungle Out There
Petting Zoo

Notes

Are you looking at a friend's book?
If you would like your own copy, send the
following order form.

Quick Order Form

Please send ____ copy(s) of
2,001 Top Titles & Tips to:

Name:_____

Address: _____

City:_____State:_____Zip:_____

Telephone:_____

Include *$14.95* per book
plus *$2.00* each for shipping and
handling and this order form. Send to:

ClearSky Publishing
P.O. Box 606-B
Hixson, TN. 37343

Tennessee residents, add 8.25% sales tax